What contemporaries are saying about EROica

In these deeply personal poems, love is a benediction to the liminal spaces of our existence where hope and despondency meet to collaborate. These poems are rhythmic and direct, often comforting the Beloved in poems such as "to an image":

> "and how can eyes capture the truth of steel
> forged in the fires of desires and the liars
> who think that you are nothing more
> than the sum of some parts, easily captured
> but never held, for they have touched nothing."

We find that DeVault is touching on something perplexingly human about the mystery of love, beauty, and craft. These poems are symbols of time coalesced into the majesties of long-term devotion.

—**Dustin Pickering,**
founder of Transcendent Zero Press and author of *The 'Ophelia' Prophecies*

William F. DeVault's Eroica astounds. This collection reaches and achieves heights of language and content beyond any that I have ever read. The table of contents itself is a work of art. Reading this collection is like spending time in a sunny Arab garden with the proverbial basket of luscious fruit and delicious wine. Moreover, the book wraps itself in a sheath of provocative sexuality and tantalizing sensuousness. To write this caliber of work requires fortitude and brilliance, and DeVault possesses both in abundance.

DeVault, in his forward, admits his ongoing passion for Mariya Andriichuk and his tribute to her existence. To that end, he has composed a work that not only salutes her, but brings into the world an incomparable, literary triumph. There are no "…reckless incantations…" on this journey of love and admiration. The voyage lifts the reader into a rarefied region where heroic crowns exist with a "Decalogue of Heroism and Love." The author owns the English language, has transformed it into a vernacular of verbal surprises that underscore his meanings and focus. Images are fresh and compelling, carry the reader into a territory that has not, to my knowledge, been presented before with such originality and imagination.

> "I should like sometime
> sometime
> to be there when you wake
> and see the skies realize
> they have been counterfeiting blue
> compared to your eyes."

Such beautiful language abounds throughout the book and brings the reader very close to the passion he feels for this lady. In fact, he says, "your passion/makes me want to live forever." How can anyone deny the simplistic power of these words? Quotable lines, unique word combinations, riveting content comprise a book worth returning to more than once. This body of work has my highest recommendation. Eroica is "all I ever wanted" from a book of poetry.

—**R. Nikolas Macioci,**
author of *Stoney Seasons* **and** *City of Hammers*

The elegantly exquisite photo on the cover of William DeVault's *EROica* is but a delicacy with which to whet one's appetite for the sumptuous verbal repast enclosed within its covers.

William's work is a delectable exploration of his sensuous and sensual Multiverse in amomantic imagery. It is an imagery which chants incantations to ensorcel every fibre of one's being. His wondrous portrait of his golden-maned Mariya is exquisitely rooted in his desire, his memories, and in a saudade only a few of us understand.

As a fellow-writer of romantic poetry and the poetry of unrequited love, I can only say: WELL-DONE!

—Doc Janning,
Poet Laureate of South Euclid, Ohio

Take Beethoven and a more-enlightened Napoleon. Bring into the 21st century. Throw in extra helpings of empathy and Eros. Then bake at 425°F in a poetry oven to make the verse sizzle and steam. *Et voilà*, you have ***EROica***, the latest and perhaps greatest book yet by U.S. National Beat Poet Laureate Emeritus William F. DeVault. Plate, serve and savor. You're welcome.

—John Burroughs,
2022-23 U.S. Beat Poet Laureate and author of *Rattle and Numb*

One might expect knowing William F. DeVault's intelligent, powerful, skilled poetry that we would "Begin at the end" which we do in this volume, dedicated to Mariya Andriichuk, a friend and collaborator. William starts this poetry volume at the end and winds up in a "Sphere of Venus". Young or new authors (oldsters too) would do well to become familiar with DeVault's work as they do any author of classical renown.

—Dane Ince,
California State Beat Poet Laureate

When my friend Bill, "William F." DeVault pours out his heart, it is not just a faint trickle of broken-hearted blues. Oh no we are talking about a majestic outpouring of love and romance and shall we say just a little bit of perseverance. This is more of a water cannon of love and tribute. Never one to be a slacker, Bill reminds us of the gentle soul with the fiercest of heart. In this collection, we do not find a broken heart but one on the mend thanks to the creature that has taken his token of love, no not an ordinary token perhaps a doubloon or a golden dollar of yore. In his poem sensible horizon, he says it all:
> "I want to see beyond the edge of the world
> leaving behind the sensible horizon
> to reach for all I ever wanted, all that haunted me."

—Larry Jaffe,
Florida State Beat Poet Laureate

EROica

William F. DeVault

ISBN-13: 9781734946994

For Mariya, who gave me back my life.

.

Table of Contents

Foreword

This is a book from me unlike any you have read before.

Oh, it is poetry, with a flourish of styles and language and intensity…but the difference is the focus. Having a lifetime of poetry in which I have obscured the identities of those who have inspired me, to protect them from scrutiny and harassment (it has happened), I am focusing on and dedicating this volume to Mariya Andriichuk, my friend and Constant Collaborator who has contributed so much to the imagery and vision of my works, her photography and form taking its place in my books and other media, enhancing the vision and resonance of my works.

But more than that, I must confess a deliberate and intense affection, a passion for her. A few years ago, I even proposed marriage to her. She turned me down, and it hurt, a lot, but I'm a big boy and my heart remained fixed on her. We have remained friends and collaborators, and I retain hope that one day I will inspire in her the fire that I carry for her. In some ways it will be a measure of how competent a poet, a composer of amomancies, that I am.

More than once I have confronted the possibility that remaining steadfast in my love might mean I will live out my days alone, extending my current monastic existence for the rest of my days. It has been a choice of torments, as I am by nature a passionate romantic, and such isolation is not my preference.

But here it is, **EROica**, in part a tribute to her, in part a tribute to my passion and acknowledgement of passion for her, in part about the complexities brought on by the recent invasion of her homeland, Ukraine. I am a pacifist, but I respect the fierce determination with which her people have responded and how she has stood by them.

Mariya has featured heavily in many of my books over the 14 years since I first encountered her, but this is her tribute, revelatory as it is in how I think and feel. But also about her courage and talent as she endures the fates and tides of history.

I will make certain that she approves this introduction (she did), as I have no desire to put her in an awkward position, and the fact that you are reading this means I have sought and obtained her approval to include this introduction. I am grateful for this.

Respectfully, and with abiding love.

William F. DeVault

we begin at the end

Battered, shattered, scattered, nothing mattered
but that which the nattering precognizant memories introduced us to.
Life, on terms we know to be terminal,
yet we stall to live it,
to give it beauty, duty, the sooty aftermath
of the demon core that lays within us all
even if we are too proud to admit, aloud,
that we are given to the reckless incantations,
information flowing like red wine at the witches' sabbath,
words summoning powers that are not greater than us,
for if they were, why would they need our blistered tongues
to invoke them, to provoke them to have spoken the broken tokens
of emergence, the purging of our surging madness, the clergy of our
self-forgiveness that lives within us all to call down the heavens,
call up the girl next door to implore her
to make us something we already are,
far from the fallen nights that spindle kindling
to a fire regent, present in unpleasant peasant memories
when we accepted the lies we told ourselves
as we molded our colding natures,
featureless icons of forgotten religions
we are our own gods to.
awakening to take sips from lips between hips that slipped
past our excuses of excursions and recursive reckonings.
the overture undertakes to pass through in true mockery of our silence,
violence as in a John Burroughs poem, shouted in pouts.

sensible horizon

I want to see beyond the edge of the world
leaving behind the sensible horizon
to reach for all I ever wanted, all that haunted me
when a child, dreaming of where I would be
one day, when grown and owning my destiny.
The sun touches me and I feel it warm me.
The light like a lover's hands, never tired
of touching me to tell me of desire constant.
The heat, like earnest words and thoughts
given to me to bear me to the edge of the world,
to the sensible horizon, where there you wait.

in the hall of mirrors

she's got broken memories
and broken vows
she's iconoclast to the last
against the sacred cows
she's got golden hair
that captures golden light
and lays against her naked skin
in the darkest, silent night

a lady and a lover
a princess and a muse
enigma to the complicated
but not wishing to confuse

she's powered to perfection
but knows her every flaw
when in the hall of mirrors
she's the priestess of the law

nature rests

under packed snows, nothing grows,
but there is the patience of nature
waiting the first stray beam of light
or breeze warmer than the doomed ice
to awaken the world, one deep breath at a time.
such as it is with all things of life
all things of beauty and the dreams
that are peculiar to the earth spirits
that bind heaven and hope to the ground
and will be rewarded for their magnificence.

vulnerable

she is so delicate, so frail,
and yet she has wings that let her sail
far and across the weeping sky,
something impossible for you or I
unless we release our fears,
and struggle free of our cocoons of tears
that wrap and sap and trap and bind,
vulnerable to those who find
sport in making pain for beautiful things
that by their very nature have wings
they can never touch or have or hold
their wings unearned, their spirits, cold.

like a lost soul in a cathedral

I should like sometime
sometime
to be there when you wake
and see the skies realize
they have been counterfeiting blue
compared to your eyes.

To watch you stretch
and hear you sigh as light trespasses
across your face
your neck your breasts
and lends warmth to make the morning
more palatable.

I should like sometime
sometime
to see you pad away to find breakfast
even if it is only a casual thing
with no real nutrition
just you, waking, taking time.

You would be so very
so very
beautiful that I would be silent
like a lost soul in a cathedral
and smile to myself at my redemption.

I should like sometime
sometime
to wake up next to you and ask
myself if this is real or if
I died last night and you are my God.

pink rose

the rose is soft pink,
like your lips in shaded light
as I kiss them, as they
whisper wishes I am bound to grant,
scant moments in the future
and for as long as you would have me.
my resistance has passed away
and I am cast away from all
but the pink rose of your lips,
of your hips, and that slips into me
as I slip into you,
binding me to everything made irrelevant
by the single blossom
and the petals that fill my senses,
shatter my defense,
and draw me into your garden.

Golden Gates of Kiev

You are my golden gates.
Standing tall, but not a wall against desire.
Passion of a thousand years, tears and triumph
laid inside you to draw my into mystery
the history of your love and touch.

I am just a curious onlooker to your past
wanting to cast my lot with futures yet unborn,
warm and deep inside you, finding truth, binding
my life and dreams to the arch of your body
as I enter you to find the splendour of you.

You are my golden gates.
Heroic even if I never stand in your shadow
or lay my hands to the warm stone of your needs,
needs that would feed on all I am and let me record
history in my words, adding to your legend.

A Prayer for Life and Love

Soul to dreams, dreams to thoughts and reveries
I cannot always explain in words and tricks of light.
A touch, a kiss, a prayer for life and love that sees
further than the withered sedge and edge of a night
never wasted, for it sustained me to this moment
that I might catch that spark of the divine in you,
a flicker of a soul so radiant it hides deep to prevent
those who are unworthy from reaching for it, a view
or echo of the essence of angels buried in the tapestry
where the casual observer may miss it, lost in tracing
only the patterns they can comprehend. Missing beauty,
real beauty, more than mere flesh that sends blood racing
with the acknowledgment that you are not just beautiful,
but a path into seven Heavens in a kiss of the spiritual.

open shadow

I would center you in my universe
enter you as oft as you allow,
finding you warm and hungry
for the purging, merging moments
when I am deep inside you and you ride,
ride me to my release, ceaseless
as you are beautiful and your eyes
and thighs hold me deep inside you.
unwilling to leave, wanting only
to go deeper in all ways, hearing you
as you feel my thrust and cry out,
captured by your beautiful heart
and the lips and hips that part
to take me in and make me your own.
I want to wake you, take you,
and forsake even my own sanity
for the vanity of making love
to so perfect an open shadow
of all I have had dark dreams of.

life is a gallery of art

Life is a gallery of art
and I can walk down the halls
admiring the creative hand
that mixed the colours and laid stroke
upon stroke
upon stroke
to bring the curve alive in the face
and hands
and hips
of a beautiful woman
without stealing the canvas
and running home with it
to hide it away in hunger or pride.
most of the time.

I respect the artist and the sculptor.
Rodin has always been a favourite,
able to make stone awaken
to the point that jealous hearts
accused him of casting from corpses,
for they were of the blood of Salieri
and could not comprehend
the gifts of another, envious
and bitter, their suns eclipsed
by a greater light that stole
their place on pedestals they carved
in their lust for recognition
and their willingness to believe
that they were the only stars.

I have my own definition of art
as that which resonates with me
and makes me feel something more
than a mere impression of skill,
a thrill, a chill, a will to change
and rearrange the priorities of life
or at least to know a new appreciation
for women with freckles or red hair.
It is there, in the gallery,
where we find our quickened pulses caught
in gossamer and summer wind that spins us

into hearts like pinwheels, shiny toys
that bring the smile of a child
for whom all of life is a miracle of creation.

fire

flint to steel
is not what I feel
but the soft ignition...
the red touch of tongues
of flame that rise from inside
to lick the air about me.
fire. born of desire.
immolating me.
absorb the heat.
magnify it, sanctify it
with your touch.
enter the furnace
already hot, caught in coals stirred
by a single word and a perfect kiss.
flesh that could melt stone
and bring a frozen heart to burn.
consume me in a plume of passion
share the infernal beauty of my love.

death before birth

awake my soul
hatched and patched
matched to future visions
where I have found paths fresh
like grass at the sun's first kiss,
wet with life and faith in memories
yet to be made, but welcome.

golden suffering

the silent moments when I am screaming
inside
to be touched and held, felled by my heart.
the sunrise is touching me
places where I would have you touch
but you are not here
and I fear I will love the sun
as it burns me, turns me into light
the golden suffering of needing you
to hold me, gold in your arms,
my body the horizon to your dawn.

the sum of your parts

you are more than the sum of your parts.
the some of your parts summed up in a wolf whistle
and a stranger's stare.

you are more than the lies you've been told.
petty, unpretty words that are absurd but cling
to your heart with barbed bites.

you are more than doubt and desire.
more than you will ever accept, exceptions rare
to the rule we believe the lies easier.

never tired to pray

My sins are my own and I will atone for them
in time. My fading thoughts will be caught
on fingers worn from guilt and penance,
my eyes shaded by the faded senses
and I will find my voice to raise to the heavens.

to an image

you are more than the sum of parts
too easily captured in light and word,
cut and pasted and wasted
when they do not tell the story
or even the cover of the book.

there is purpose to the person,
and every vision provisioned of hope
tells us more than the curve of skin
and the colour of your hair.
fair though you may be, you are more.

for every soul wears the shell of life,
every life wears the shell of experience,
and every experience is more than fate,
more than random chance and happenstance.
it is the forge of the soul, the furnace.

and how can eyes capture the truth of steel
forged in the fires of desires and the liars
who think that you are nothing more
than the sum of some parts, easily captured
but never held, for they have touched nothing.

to an angel

I shall pour out my essence on the dark water
that you may draw it into the wounds
cut by the unworthy hands that dare touch
what they could not deserve.

if I must wither and die that you may fly,
then I shall smile and go out happy.
there is a time to all purposes and things,
but to give wings to an angel would be beautiful.

and I would rather die a beautiful death
than draw breath in a world where angels
fear to fly and draw awe from the faithful
who always wanted to see an angel, as I have.

happy of the happiest

I am free to be myself
to reconnect with who I am and was
and always will be, when allowed
to feel proud of my roots
and my family
and my memories of the old stone wall
I used to lean against
when I spoke to you
of what I would be when I grew up.

my town

like something out of myth and lore
where dreams are spun of distant shore
and mountains yet to find and best
to put your passions to the test
and mark your life from here to there
but never lose the wistful stare
that bids a smile and begs a tear
of places ever held so dear.

hair power

Like Rapunzel in reverse,
you curse the wind
and have sinned against all the lesser lovelies,
their chemically-twisted,
misted masses trashed
and crashed while you let down your hair
and it rises to the occasion,
a banner of beauty
and tender care that fills the air
with the dreams of mortal men,
wishing to wake in the tangle of your jungle.

crucified

worship me with more that your kisses
for I have had that shallow touch
and know the unreached depths cry "Martyr",
begging for more. for all. and still more.
worship me with more than your senses
for I have found the lost spectrum
deep inside me, crying out in crucifixion
to pain of taking less than what I need.
worship me with more than memory
for I have not gone anywhere
you cannot touch and kiss and sense
and I would be worthy of your prayers.

The 1st heroic crown of Mariya

1: eyes of glass

An elegant beauty, eyes of glass and silvered
like visions captured now in a digital age,
caged in frames to lay immortal, white, black or red,
the pale pinks and greys of flesh and fantasy, sage
thoughts unspoken for the thousand word proxies caught
and projected to distant voyeurs, the silent
partners in a dance of your soul, flying and fraught
with consequence that slips away like a serpent.
You own your dreams, and barter them for ovations
and more material things. This is the nature
of a true artist, remembered after nations
rise and fall and call out to histories, unsure.
Your images, no matter kisses made, tears wept,
mirrors that retain their images, visions kept.

2: visions kept secret and secure

Mirrors that retain their images, visions kept
secret and secure. Dreams erotic and impure
are prayed away, the debris of yesterday swept
into the street and the new petals emerge, sure
that they are the prettiest flower. And they are,
for new life, new tender traces, these are beauty.
Every morning you rise and prize our bright star
as an omen of the promise of a duty
to find your vision in shuttered winks, never far
from yourself. You are more beautiful than the sun,
and yet you know the eclipse, and the night, they are
always part of your world, given but never won.
Day to night and you drink in what was done or said
as forever as light, as night, as earnest bled.

3: Alexandrite

As forever as light, as night, as earnest bled
by shallow, sallow lovers, brittle stone and bone
passing for alexandrite and sapphire, fear fed
the specter of solitude, of being alone.
I shall not desert you. I shall never hurt you
by intention or mention meant to represent
false feelings or facades that promenade in rue
of lost times and past crimes for which we now repent.
I would merge and purge and surge and emerge from you
reborn a better man, to give all that I am,
tribute to all I would ask in simplest hope, true
to your word and kiss and touch against those who damn
me for my love and loyalty, a lost concept
as prayer on the lips of a woman, words wept.

4: Words wept

As prayer on the lips of a woman, words wept.
No miracle, merely a repurposed pilgrim
seeking something more than mediocrity kept
in cold shadows, held in failed light to fade and dim
as a mistaken memory. I want, desire,
an holy fire. As mortal soul may reach for God
I reach for her, with the truth she can inspire
within me, revelation that evens the odd
cobblestones on a path that leads into her heart.
If the divine is in all things, then in my lust
I find sacred blossoming and rebirth part
and sum of my affections, not a graven dust.
I have dreamed of her in scriptures for her to bless.
I have dreamed of her in midnight kiss and caress.

5: Midnight kiss and caress

I have dreamed of her in midnight kiss and caress.
Exotic, the erotic possibilities
beyond my imagination, for tenderness
and urgency merge in a perfect heat, to please
her in sharp moments and sleepless nights, the delights
that would shock satyrs and sate each wish and need
is a command and demand of my passions, flights
of worship of her limbs and form and warm, wet mead
I would consume into a drunken stupor, voice
to brave and wicked utterances in the tongues
of forgotten religions, idolatry's choice
of our histories and mysteries to be sung.
I would be the priest, temple tender to her fires.
I have seen her conquering the world as she requires.

6: Awe

I have seen her conquering the world as she requires.
Small corners taken from the darkness, vast vistas
overcome with the sweep of her hand, she inspires
awe in those capable of perceiving the laws
of a universe she is free to bind to her,
to make bend and flow and go her way, she is strong.
When she believes, she weaves tapestries to ensure
that all memory reflects her perspectives, long
after she is gone, she will linger in the hearts
of those who see the beauty she had seen and caught
in the faery nets of digitized silver, parts
of a mosaic of her laugh and smile and thought.
But not greater than her beauty, I must confess.
Sleek and slender, tender heart my passions to bless.

7: Tender heart my passions to bless

Sleek and slender, tender heart my passions to bless.
Reaching out to God, seeking a permanent peace
with the divine to find the truth and the noblesse
obligation to give of herself a release
to share her heart and soul in a colder world, grey
except when the tulips bloom too rare, too rare to
fill every day with their palette and to stay
as guardians and heralds of joy made anew
every day, every way. Snow is welcome
only for a season, only for a reason
in her street corners and window boxes, made numb
by the cold wind and colder hearts, the freedom
to be seeking sanctuary in her desires.
Holy water, her sweat anoints the sacred fires.

8: Nazarite's hair

Holy water, her sweat anoints the sacred fires.
I would bathe in this purifying sheen, made clean,
the purity of her darkest pleasures, desires
to a purpose and to the moment, visions seen
a thousand times, the cascade of Nazarite's hair
that falls as veil that fails to hide her rare beauty.
Dreams invoked and provoked, words spoken to the air
in hopes that God listens to hopeless prayers, duty
of supplicant and paramour, seeking heaven
in her touch and kiss, to be the missionary
positioned to enter the temple, no heathen,
but believer seeking to merge without tarry.
To be the lover ordained to her dreams and needs.
To be the father of her children, to plant seeds.

9: To plant seeds

To be the father of her children, to plant seeds.
A contemplation and consummation to love.
How many are so blinded by her that their needs
are far simpler. Far less ambitious, nothing of
the need to do more than see her beauty, frozen
in frame and to dream in liquid frustrations, held
at a distance by their own cowardice. Chosen
dreams that objectify her elegant heat, welled
as tears of pale sorrow to their own failed courage.
Delicate derisions and sour grapes to shield
fragile egos, they stare and dare nothing, they rage
and blurt guttersnipe appreciations, revealed
as shadow hearts, daring naught, never to ensure
joy and awe, the law of a prophet transfigured.

10: Transfigured

Joy and awe, the law of a prophet transfigured.
I watch you dance and see the grace of an angel.
The curve and swerve as you move me, so self-assured,
knowing that I must look, caught up as the stars fell.
You became the heavens in my heart long before
I could confess it in manner but clever song.
Your pout shouts and your smile is evidence and more
that there is a God behind the scenes, making wrong
into the kindness of your very existence.
You are worthy of adoration, of a grace
more than most can ever comprehend, persistence
of a melody as ancient as time to place
offerings on the altar to your released needs.
Grace in a place of madness, a sadness that bleeds.

11: In a place of madness

Grace in a place of madness, a sadness that bleeds
pain and stain and the grain of rough roads, the burden
that can take you, break you, make your rosary beads
worn and torn and shorn of meaning. Uncertain
yesterdays and the question of light, bright beacons
or a subtler shade. Draw into sharp relief lines
that define our divinity. Dead eyed deacons
preaching their own religions, never serving wines
of a Holy Land where you stand, an artist's heart
brings forth revelation in the transmutation
of a beautiful woman into icon, part
of a plan to a sensual resurrection.
The vessels of our communion, we are assured,
warm wine and white blood, a soft surrender deferred.

12: Soft surrender deferred

Warm wine and white blood, a soft surrender deferred.
Take me to your bedchamber, I will anoint you with attars
I brought with me from the furthest corners of conscience, cured,
passed through the sunlight and the moonlight and the stars
wise, as my intent is both pure and plutonic,
I am consumed with passion for your bright beauty,
elegant, exceptional, sweet and ironic
that I am captured to pay a perfect duty
as hostage to your murmured sadness and the sweet,
for you are greater than I am, Hephaestus bound
to your Aphrodite, a bold acolyte daring to compete
for that which he could never be worthy, of, found
as foundation to what I most desire this night,
to love the lady with the eyes that capture light.

13: Eyes that capture light

To love the lady with the eyes that capture light.
Now there is a path that I would gladly follow,
happily walking, shadow or rain, day or night.
We are born to love the worthy that fill, hollow,
the center of our souls, where we mislaid the faiths
to believe in perpetual passion and fire
that there are those who can and will dismiss the wraiths
if we let them in with open heart and conspire
with the angels themselves to make a place of peace
where we may dare and share and care to fulfill life
against the hell others wallow in without cease.
We are made to rise above the pain and the strife,
we are made to dance and love and seek for the light,
to dream of memories to be made in the night.

14: Memories to be made in the night

To dream of memories to be made in the night.
To think of you, wrapped around me like second skin,
whispering your most wicked will for the delight
that you will never leave, never allow the sin
of sharing such intimacies with another,
holding nothing back. The hunger and fantasies
that you deserve to fulfill, lady and mother,
courtesan and princess, whatever would most please
your needs and make you but more hungry for my blood,
with smile and kiss and curve of that prehensile tongue,
I will listen for your subtle direction, flood
you with my essence, that all your sweet songs are sung
in my arms, cradled and enabled, my delight:
To dream of memories to be made in the night.

15: The Diadem

An elegant beauty, eyes of glass and silvered
mirrors that retain their images, visions kept
as forever as light, as night, as earnest bled
as prayer on the lips of a woman, words wept.
I have dreamed of her in midnight kiss and caress.
I have seen her conquering the world as she requires.
Sleek and slender, tender heart my passions to bless.
Holy water, her sweat anoints the sacred fires.
To be the father of her children, to plant seeds,
joy and awe, the law of a prophet transfigured,
grace in a place of madness, a sadness that bleeds
warm wine and white blood, a soft surrender deferred.
To love the lady with the eyes that capture light.
To dream of memories to be made in the night.

Mariya

I do not mind
the wicked curve and swerve
of your hips
your slender limbs and tender lips.
But the sexiest part of you is your soul.

Mariya

chocolate nostalgia

your skin glistens
as the night listens
listens for a memory
nostalgic for the touch
the pleasure
the infinite measure
of a moment caught
and held, hot and taut,
inside

passion, sepia

the look in eyes
where passion reigns
and the pain of hollow hours
is shattered by a touch that extends into all corners,
born of flesh,
borne on spirit
and burned into my memory
by the merest thought of you,
hot with hunger and desire,
a goddess of fire
made avatar for the worship of her.
a religion of needs,
bleeding as sacrament
from one into another
until there is no more solitude.
your passion
makes me want to live forever.

one more day without you

One more day without you
and the sun dries my tears,
the night is torment and torture,
the sheets mocking me with memory.

One more day without you
and I live outside of time,
straddling yesterday and tomorrow,
places where you dwell for now.

One more day without you
and I shall fold my hopes
and all the promises you made
and trust you from necessity.

yielding to temptation

yielding to your fantasies.
skies don't lie and I,
I am caught in your cotton candy kisses,
held soft and aloft
like a prayer that dares eyes to caress
each curve with nervous nakedness
of heart and satin skin,
thin to the osmosis of dreams.
yielding to temptation,
crossing boundaries that bind
and blind me to my promises to be good.
bare feet on infinite sheets of sand
that are more than just a place
to trace our illusions,
the winds whipping us to crown senses drowned
in the elegant whispers
that remind us of what we really yield to.

life is easy as a plumelet

ah to be a feather,
brushed across warm skin,
eliciting gooseflesh.
the better to savour the thin
membrane between your being
and my ticklish presence.
wanting nothing more than
to have you brush your sense
of touch once more with my plume,
proud risen by your sensuousness
and the joy I find in your smile
and the soft skin against which I press.

with guitar

play to me the memories you would have me recall,
my strings eager for your fingers and the breath
of your voice and choice to be with me tonight.

six strings making love out of the tension in them,
the echoes of their song die but leave memories
of a beautiful woman taking the time to share life.

play to me the memories you would have me recall,
my strings eager for your fingers and the breath
of your voice and choice to be with me tonight.

seen through objective eyes

seen through subjective eyes
you have a grace of form that a man
(such as myself) cannot help but admire
and feel a desire to express
in word or look or touch or more
if given opportunity to live a dream.
for I am not a camera, I am a man,
bound by the sound of the my own heart
pounding and resounding to see you
standing proud and naked to the light,
seen through the objective eye of a camera
that stands as proxy for my admiring eyes.

fire inside

the sky waits, radiant blue,
for the red you bring with your fire
and I wait, wait for you,
burning with kindled desire.

you burn in colours of a raging soul,
infrared to heat sweetly and completely
consume those brave enough to touch
the flame without shame, moths to die,
frying in a split/second agony of joy
at having found the essence of you.

the sky waits, radiant blue,
for the red you bring with your fire
and I wait, wait for you,
burning with kindled desire.

after space exploration

after all the corners of the universe
have been safely seen, cataloged and mapped,
there will be a sense of sorrow,
for the mysteries will be gone.
to some people's way of thinking.

but, after space exploration,
the infinite skies of the human heart
will still remain, begging our resolve
to see what is out there and in there,
a beauty beyond the stars and skies.

God's care

Were that I were God
to be able to hold you
in the palm of my hand
as you slept
dreaming of things I would only see
through your eyes and life.
To protect you from skinned knees
and the inevitable broken hearts.
To send the cooling breeze
on a hot summer's day
and to smile, invisible,
as you go on your way
content in the knowledge
that if I were God, you'd never
skin a knee, unless you wanted to.
and the angels would accept
that I love you above all creation.

Diamond Cuts Diamonds

the light dances across familiar terrain.
your skin in the window
calling forth the golden lover
bound forever by the laws of nature
to stand at a distance
but able to draw pleasure from your beauty
and return some small measure
in the tongues of warmth and comfort
it plays and lays upon your shoulders
and breasts and back and face and legs
caresses from a not-indifferent lover
but one bound like Prometheus
to an aching fate while all the while
craving the touch of your hand
and to seek new places to play and lay
and hide itself away, to only give comfort
to you, that you may know the intimacy
you inspire in the desire of the sun.

Thinking of God

I find evidence of God
in the way you smile.
proof positive, that there is
something undefiled
despite the way the world spins,
often trashing hopes.
for you have that essence, prime,
surmounting slopes
that lead to the mountaintop
where there is vision
that sees beyond the moment
and finds in us one
more chance to dance with bare feet
on the soft Spring grass
and laugh like children
as the angels pass.

I still smell the sweet metallic taste of your skin

I still smell the sweet metallic taste of your skin
fresh from the shower
the power you held over me is undiminished
locking me away from other gardens
no pardons or a free pass
to indulge elsewhere
my ravenous thirst and cursed
as I am by my desire you your fire
to melt this coeur rage cage
I have found and bound myself
until such time as you give a kiss
to unlock the cell, or to find the moment
to shatter my gaol with an incandescent
transfiguration from man to angel to deva.

46 minute villanelle: the futility of truth

Truth is but a frail metaphor inspired.
The illusion born of an obsession
desired, admired, ultimately required.
A quote is not truth, merely attired
in finery of eloquence, passion.
Truth is but a frail metaphor inspired.
The best we hope for is a kiss, tired
of the touchless seductions flushed ashen.
Desired, admired, ultimately required.
The solemn experience we acquired
tells tales, shadow puppetry compassion:
Truth is but a frail metaphor inspired.
Peace is good. Love, as well, sold and satired
by shadow poets, speaking in fashion
desired, admired, ultimately required.
All roads: Entropy. Futility sired
by the myths and legends of perfection.
Truth is but a frail metaphor inspired.
Desired, admired, ultimately required.

She was Skyclad

She was skyclad
bare to the night
a light unto herself
and the sweet heat
radiated permeated consecrated
the wind as it slid along her form
my warm hands ached to follow suit
beneath the clouds
against her shoulders
and the moon granting
pale blue light
across her breasts and hair
as she assented to my passion
if only in my most wicked dreams

Woman

The essence of grace and discernment.
The only reason the human race
made it this far.
Evidence that God is not a man
found in the blessing of creation
and the power of her love.

Last Night in Paradise

Dance with me, foregoing the artifice,
lovers on the verge of more than a kiss.
The moment made of cream and strawberries.
The pretense-perfect music that carries
an intoxicating rhythm and flow
that supposes that we know what we know
when the mysteries remain on the floor
and the linen cocoon finds nevermore
our vanities, ascendant to great light
transfigured in the darkness of the night.

it is snowing in Kyiv

it is snowing in Kyiv
the frozen tears of angels
falling soft upon your skin
as proxy for my kisses

transcending the darkness

if we survive this night
then we shall live forever
the fire having proven our metal and mettle
the breathless drowned downs of criminal kisses
and the knowledge carved in our legacies
what need will we have of yesterday
then all the impatient futures freeze our disease
of solitude and sorrow
the last supper transfiguring our blood and flesh
and making breakfast a meal of championed dreams
the shower running thick with whispers
we can only allude to, now that the prelude
is complete
and life begins
if we survive this night

Possessing me

Possessing me by taking me into secret channels
of spiritual, intellectual, creative, and carnal intimacy.
Opening all the ways to drain my resistance,
reward my persistence in solferino revelation, mysteries, and ecstasies.
Wrapped in your heart, thoughts, and hungry lips and legs
to beg a consummation demanded to seal
with sacred solemnity and rare pleasure
a baptism of sweat and wet acceptance
of pulsing sacrifice of flesh.

Possessing me

Epithets and sobriquets

Epithets and sobriquets.
So many I have carried,
Like a married woman's name,
Reshaped to drape a new image
When the old one was fine.
I would love to know the words
And tone of voice you use
When you choose to speak of me.

defining you

You are
an impossibly perfect dream
And every fiber of my existence cries out for you to be mine,
Yet, I know that I am
far from first in line to your heart. But that is what dreams are for.
That is what you were born to,
To be creator and muse,
Mirror and light
The bright bustle of noonday
And the pleasures of the night.

the tenor clears his throat

justifying evil in the name of righteousness.
are people really that vain and foolish?
I grieve
the loss
of love and respect
for the rights of the victims
for the rights of women
for the fallen soldiers
wasted for the old men's ego and greed
coddling madness and death
spoil those spoiling to prove their legacies
their masked masculinities
with the blood of others
as we twist in a wind
that was here before the people came
to game their survival while selling their souls
to the basest of lies and shoddy assumptions
the consumption of our hearts
the depravity and death of the
human race

Decalogue of Heroism and Love

I.

Heroism is manifest in existence
rising and falling and rising to the calling
of that which is necessary
not just for yourself
but for those who need heroes,
champions and icons
cut of flesh and stone and bone
and blood. all the blood shed to the
effigies of mystery and history
for the trouvere to reflect and expect
at least a little respect for recounting
to the hearts of future dreamers.

II.

To dare to love is an act of purest heroism
the schism of the prism of earnest light,
split into the infinite bandwidths,
the better to realize that all truths
are given to both perspective and perception,
the conception of tombstone
the blasphemy uttered by gods and prophets.

III.

Remember us to yesterday, closing the circle
In infinite recursion, the perversions of hope
that rope us into self-justification, prayers
pricked in the shattered glass of the mirrors
that delight us not, caught to trammel us
in inelegant poses, blistered roses fed slaughterhouse
leavings, left as debris, but upon which
we find the bindings and blindings made kindling
for future pyres, hard-wired by false faiths
that trap us in the tiniest of boxes.

IIII.

I remember our first kiss. Lip to lip,
long before hip to hip was even a thought
caught up in my fantasies, playing at innocence
as self-defense, pretense unconscious
as the preconscious gathered ash and embers
to be remembered for the coming famines,
the colder ages and cages of metals
made of allied alloys that spoil us
into thinking we can do no wrong,
strong with the convections of our fictions
as we trade frictions in fractions.

V.

tonight
men and women and children so young we do not
differentiate their genders
are dying.
some by natural causes, some of the unnatural
whims of the monsters born to others.
murder, rape, genocide, for pride of country
or clan, evil and the smiles of senile old men
trying to prove they still have power or prayers
of leaving a legacy in the unmarked graves.

VI.

I will make of you an immortal goddess,
for I perceive the possibilities inherent,
apparent, the apparition in the sunlight,
bending light, unending, the infinite renewal
that is the nature of all things, crystal facets
seen in eyes of stained glass and fire,
desire and surrender, the never-ending release
from the gray moments others remind us of,
loveless creatures and features the teachers
of mediocrity recite to us from their graves.
the caves, hollow and monstrous, echoes
off the walls unseen but ever-present.

VII.

Lay with me for a season, your reasons are your own
but time has shown the illusions come and go, as you will,
memories that encase you and embrace you,
the poisons are our own, we lie in mediocrities
as we cannot face the epic and heretic truths —
that we are heirs to legends. lovers that cover
the ground between the temples with words and passions.

VIII.

I am sincere in drawing near, here
where you fear my presence, caught and tormented
by the glib sibilance of pretty strangers
whose monuments will fade and fall
to leave behind little but the muck of self-deception
written in endorphins and steroids,
the plasticity of ephemeral play
in the gardens of the immortal.
this is the reality, I carry it with me,
whether you can stand to admit
to your best state of being, I announce it.
until you move along.

VIIII.

In the gossamer we are trapped and captured,
cured of uncertainty unless we are so bound
by our religion of self-deprecation that we must
trust the lies that despise what we could be
should be would be if we awoke to the light
of a baptismal sun, running like children
in the cleansing rain, washing away stain
as we strain to know all that we were meant to know.

X.

Marry me before you bury me, I am not immortal,
but an impure and durable heart that will notch
the walls of the temple for the wonderment
of passing pilgrims and the dreams of the damned
who did not have to give up so soon. So soon.

parse this face

Parse this farce into bite-sized bits of bitterness
and the sweet salvation of your jasmine realms,
brought to mind on honeysuckle breezes wafting
me aloft in the resurrection of perfection denied.
Everything in everything and nothing of note left
behind like yearbooks in a casket, I am still angry
over that. I won't deny it, but water under a bridge
I have crossed ten thousand times and my crimes
are not negligible. Constantly performing penances
you will never understand, like earnest prayers sent
inward as God is everywhere, even in me. Free
to remember, to break apart like a candy heart wasted
in the tasted prelude to transfiguration, burst,
cursed, and made to be the last of the first, wait
for me in London or New York, or even in the shadows
of a Venice I will not forget, emblem branded to show
your ownership, if it is your will and whim, your choice
for I am just a voice, whispering your name at night.

EROica in white leather and lace

the tonic key is fluids meshing with locks burst asunder.
elegance and eloquence not mutually exclusive
considered observation as that small spider continues the hunt
for pathways not yet webbed thoroughly. organic iron, sticky
with need and greed, trapping what is necessary and sometimes
merely the collateral damage, inedible or out of the range
of the hunter's woven bindings. finding less in more like nuance
lost in the haiku of simplicity. stardust and earth's crust
kicked skyward by the skyclad ladies offering a silencing of madness,
the fear of death forgotten for hours of flowers consumed
in the plowed under garden, pardon for sins imagined and made
part of the mythology in fact, for not all legends are deceit.
the amomancies are called for and left behind in grind and slide,
denied too long to see if the tantalus of tapestries is braided
in gold and ruby-blue threads of spun sapphires, the desires
that are not extinguished by time, but by satiation.
the tonic key is fluids meshing with locks burst asunder.

Song of the ether and the sky

From first photon that struck my eyes,
you mesmerized me.
Beyond mere beauty,
there was an inescapably draw of a gravity of first water,
pulling me down,
bartering for my words without you even knowing I existed.
The fireflowers fell
in twisting cascades
the metaphors leapt from soul to mind to lip to page
faster than I could inscribe,
losing (no doubt) many verses and pages.
The couer-rage cages trapped me
I was bound by sinew and long, long, long hair
that wrapped about me
drew me in to a death spiral to the next life.
Your soul, flying, lifted me, gifted me
with lost immolation and resurrections.
the immortal song was reborn
worn like the silks of an impossible wedding bed.

beyond the gates

incandescent arms to guard and guide us
in the 4 dimensions that constitute reality.
the theory and theology of lovers,
banished and vanished
from the shadows that
bound, surround, and confound others
who dare not burn at a heat beyond fire.
plasma and the purity of a heat
both alien and reassuring.
a fragment of a poem mourned until it finds
a way to build upon doubt and uncertainty
free of the gravity of a blue-white sphere
where we are near enough to count the moments.
the hours. the days. the months. the years.
the lifetimes between touches
and the validation
of consecration and creation.
sacramental wine of a religion of those who chose
to live beyond the comfort of conformity.
to care, to dare, to share, to touch, to kiss, to coit.

Shared breath, small death, Evidence of life and love

inhale what has already passed through my lungs and tongue
and return it to me, with your assent and consent
to acknowledge that we have purified what had died
in the pollution of nations and corporations

love is not born in the boardroom and the war room
but is mocked and eviscerated until we touch the wind
and master in our own surrender the nuance
of the dance of the zephyr and hurricane

small breaths, shared deaths
evidence of life and hope

capture my soul as you share control of this chimera
born of our desire and dreams, inhaling life
and exhaling the doubt of yesterdays
prana nirvana and the sensation of warm breath

unforgiven

amomancies dance on the fingertips of the poets and lovers
(not always one and the same) for faith of the amourists as they
pour out their divine wine on the ground, seeking redemption
and the curious cachet that passes so often for what it is not
when bent and sent in the moment passing, massing like dark armies
in the night when we are most lonely. I have lived, unforgiven,
as I write my epistles to the believers, vespers whispered and wrought
on the loom of precognizant memory. woven of earnest whimsy,
words spoken and oaths broken, but the vigil is venerable.
When the light extinguishes itself, I will wait in the dark
Until flesh fails and I learn the limits of the power of my will
as I carry this temple of Aphrodite with me to the place of skulls.

sunflower fields in time of war

the sunflower fields where you ran as a child bear the scars of metal and fire
made by self-righteous murderers seeking to crush, to pillage each village
each highway with their thinly cloaked hobnail boots, blistering history
in the greed and need for self-justification, this creation ill-suited for polluted
hearts and souls, ghouls and fools killing children and feigning outrage
when their parents and brothers and sisters dare to strike back.

in the darkness be the light

there is nothing more to be said, when everyone wants heroes and heroics,
as they are but mortals, and all souls are incandescent, infused with the same
divine energy and essence. we are taught we are needful of rescue even
when we are quite capable of standing on our own, speaking our truths
in the face of opposition and the desecration of fear and doubts, shouting
like the Santa Ana Winds, blowing in heat and ionizations to blister sinister
scars across us and obscuring our paths as they blind our eyes. the light
is within you, and while there is nothing wrong with sharing our lights
we must be ever aware that we are self-sufficient to our lives, capable
of miraculous acts and the assemblage of reality from desperate dreams.

I send you the starlight

I send you the starlight, as well as the sun.
the moon reflects photons in a cold, comforting glow.
the heavens are the fields of the flowers of night
planets flitting from point to point in seasons of dreams.
you are in the firmament, beautiful, immortal, divine
by all measures, treasure of truth, pleasure, time and space.

epic/the mock battlefield

sunflowers burning in the chemical rain as metaphor for souls lost
crossed off tallies in balance sheets for the bounties paid to mercenaries
for who killed the most children and raped the most schoolgirls
a brutal world where cowardice is confused with courage
we all know our ignorances to be truths because we cannot face
the disgrace the shame the blame of never accepting fundamental
wisdom that life and love and hope are stronger than any steel
harder and hotter than any bullet more explosive than any missile
in the expediences of the battlefield, the cattle calls to mock vespers
so that we can feel good about the evil we do in the name of country
in the name of leaders who never risk their own asses just the youth
of their fatherland to die inside if not in totality for the sins of old men.

epic/the true battlefield

within you beats a tick tock heart
I have heard it
ear pressed against your breasts
the relentless fueling and purification of your body soul mind
drummer to the marching of your multicoloured mind binding
experience inspiration imagination glass eyes to capture the moments
held in an uncertain suspension of disbelief relief the chief
vanguard of tomorrow built in prickly sticks on the scaffolds of folding dreams
killing time by making immortality out of moments
your virtual vision precision to the chaos of the folded world
as you take every brisant bitter moment and crumbled idol
to make something new better besting the even indwelling critics.

and so we begin

pictures of an exhibitionist, graceful beautiful, her father's pride
at the ability to make colours of the grey dusty world curled
around like the Midgaard serpent spent in mythologies mysteries
rituals in bright patchwork prayers memories. near miss in a kiss
and tears from so far away they are dryer that dust before the wind
can bear their scent to me to wash away the best intentions
inventions of a girl growing to womanhood as food for her own
dreams of what that means in the fullness of time rhyme that dances
in pastels places while the lights flicker in neon tapers distant
and momentary at best. lies told to you told to yourself
to keep away the fear of mediocrity and the ordinary good
that will never be great but by sheer will and talent relenting
nothing in the tides of time to be the bride of illusions
confusions protruding like drunken suitors beating down
your values by bidding against themselves to convince you
that you are not better than they are all the while knowing
you are. iridescent radiant from ruddy to gold to white to blue-white light
as you establish your own heavens that make no compromise
for the lies of others that tried to pull you back keep you down
make of you less than their easy outs and gaslit streetcorners.

Plato's cave

I have never kissed your lips
entered your hips
or found a way around defenses
that confound me
perhaps by design
finding me unsuitable
or perhaps not used to something
of the magnitude I represent
in a present projected into a future
where we surpass the geometry
of body and souls at rest
who accept the colocation of consciousness
when there is ample evidence
that we are more
that what can be held
by the illusions of Plato's Cave.

in the sphere of Venus

war is born not in the sphere of Mars but the sphere of Venus
where passions flow like nitrogen lava bubbling up from within
to scald the relative ecosystems of our lives, sheltered hearts
held apart to commit indignities against ourselves, banshee cry
that dies with the next rising sun that seems too late in coming.

you and I, both, have seen, experienced, and done things we
are not proud of, but have accepted as art of the mortal path
through ice and fire, indifference and desire, tears born and borne
in many cauldrons in many corners of our minds or flesh or souls
baked into landscapes of transgressive mysteries and histories.

we only hint at our scandals and self-vandalizing actions as we
seek traction against the pull of dismay and the grave, saving
nothing for the return trip to ourselves our sought destinies
burning like an Holy bush to announce the revelation of Gods
we cannot define by the wine from water prestidigitation.

I have offered you a place at the table to feed on my experience
to know what you can cull from the harvest of my heart and art
laid bare as an Aztec offering of a brave heart to sun gods
curling around us like serpents of fire and brisant sorrows
when the pain of the vivisection of being is torn from us.

standing on the mountain, eroding into nothingness in time
as the clock ticks wicked warnings of unborn memories
stacked cracked and refracted as light through a prism
that doubles as a prism of colours we cannot define
with our limited understandings, warmth bartered coldly.

we all require allies in war against the damning nights
where we lay alone, or with those we know we should not
but we are caught in our own webs of fantasy and desperation
to not accept the blistering truth of human nature, divine hearts,
and the PTSD of romance tried pried pridefully denied to us

Selah

Acknowledgements

There will be those who make much of the shortness of this book compared to many of my volumes. The simple fact is, as is my custom, I wrote substantially more poems than made the cut and for once did not choose to circle back and, in repetition, add wave after wave of works, If the message of this book is unclear, I am not the amomancer I have been branded or the reader is incompetent.

I would like to let it be known that in addition to the aforementioned Mariya Andriichuk, dozens, perhaps hundreds, perhaps thousands, ad infinitum, have played their parts, known or unknown, in the inception and conception of this book. Those whom I have loved and who have loved me in return. You are all missed and blessed and remembered with a fierce and subtle passion that even I can barely comprehend.

Poets, artists, and artisans of stone, paint, flesh, and words have inspired me and made of me the strange and twisted creature that I endure being. An old muse once said that I was born two centuries too late or too early to be respected or understood. She was partially correct, but I always hated to argue. If she, or anyone, could live inside my brain, with all the sacrosanct madness I have learned to barely constrain, I am not so certain that the villagers would not descend on me with pitchforks and torches, and I probably wouldn't blame them.

It has been nearly two decades since I forcibly ripped myself from the mainstream of human interaction. It is a strange and lonely existence, but it was necessary for me to continue in this screaming mediocrity that is modern life. I am grateful to everyone who has made my visit gentler and more enjoyable than most, and to list the names here would take probably another hundred pages. Let's leave it at that.

About the author

"To be on the wire is life, the rest is waiting". – Karl Wallenda

The author, should the fates and the clock allow, will produce at least three more large volumes of his work with Venetian Spider Press, already under planning stages. If not, take this for what it is, a true amomancy.

Born in Greenville, South Carolina, USA, in the summer of 1955, the second of five children, DeVault grew up in an Air Force family all over the United States, living In Alaska, Washington, North Dakota, Colorado, Michigan, West Virginia, then finally when old enough to strike out on his own, has lived in Maryland, Virginia, Mississippi, and California, where he counts Venice Beach as his home.

Raised Southern Baptist, he flirted with the Episcopal faith before finding is path in the Society of Friends, Quakers, and is politically liberal by U.S. standards.

He has been married and divorced twice, fathered three remarkable children, and written enough poetry to fill a few libraries.

He doesn't collect clippings and admits to being a lousy self-promoter. He has dozens of books to his credit and has toured from Boston to Los Angeles, from Michigan to New Orleans.

He acknowledges that, by many standards he has lived a remarkable life and been lucky to a fault.

Ingram Content Group UK Ltd.
Milton Keynes UK
UKHW031218070323
418148UK00008B/385